Setting and achieving goals
and having fun!

Workbook Workout

Goal Setting & Achieving

ISBN 1453604820
EAN-13 - 9781453604823

First Printed December 2008.

Introduction...

Welcome to the new you! This workbook workout is empowering and enlightening; it challenges you to actively engage yourself and to look beyond what you already know. This book delves into who you really are. It offers questions that will empower you to access your own inner wisdom.

As a young and sensitive child, I spent much of my time with the question "Why?".

- Why did this happen?
- Why do I love?
- Why do I hurt?
- Why do I have all these questions?

Over the years, I came to learn that it is these "why" questions that offers some insight into the answers but that the answers themselves don't give me much. Knowing why something happened tended to invite my own or other people's explanations, interpretations or perceptions. Only when I started exploring "what" questions did I unlock something inside myself and see that "what" questions invite inner discovery and outer action.

In this discovery I came to understand that all the books I read and all the people I spoke to offered advice or guidance or answers. These days, there are books (and answers) on every imaginable topic. But the danger of looking to books or people for answers is that they offer a detached knowledge, a wisdom that comes to you second-hand. As a result, these sources are open to misunderstanding and your power being given to the source of the information.

This workbook asks you questions as a means for you to discover the wisdom and answers within yourself. When you find your own answers for yourself, you will come to a truer understanding and greater trust of your own power and inner guidance – a gift we seem to have lost in these frenetic and turbulent times of the information age. May this book take you one step closer the next age, the age of wisdom!

"When you find your own answers, for yourself, you will come to a truer understanding and greater trust of your own power and inner guidance"

The age of wisdom

After many years of leading, being lead, learning and teaching, I have gradually come to see the age in which we live a little differently – through eyes that are open to the wisdom that continues to grow within me. I share this workbook workout with the following in mind:

- This book is written from the point of view that you, the reader, already have all the resources, wisdom and power to create the life you love and achieve the goals to which you are committed.

- The purpose of this workbook workout is to empower and support you in accessing the wisdom and power within you and to create the life you love to live.

"The key to harnessing the power and value of this book is in your attitude and willingness to engage in questions wholeheartedly."

If you want to learn to ride a bicycle, the best way to learn is to get on the bicycle. Merely observing someone ride or reading a manual about on how to ride a bicycle is simply not enough as you probably already know ...

Putting pen to paper!

Skimming through these questions or reading them and answering them in your head is a little like reading about riding a bicycle. You may learn a lot, but nothing will prepare you for what it's really like being on that saddle – and you will end up watching the world pass by from your seat on the pavement. Your power is truly unlocked when you take time to write out what is in your head, so that you can actively engage with your own thoughts and ideas.

For each exercise in this book, and for each of the questions posed, I encourage you to take the time to write out the answers in the space provided. Relax, give yourself time and space to enjoy the gentle and unfolding journey that these questions invite.

Over time, I have come to discover that what fulfils me most is having the opportunity to make a difference to another. It is my wish that this book goes some way to enhancing the quality of your life!

With love and gratitude,

Zane Green

Acknowledgments...

It is with much gratitude that I acknowledge and thank all those of you who have supported me in the creation of www.happivate.com and this workbook.

As much as I risk leaving someone out, I feel compelled to name those that come to mind and heart as being pivotal in this creation.

Firstly, I acknowledge and thank God, the divine presence, there have been so many moments of synchronicity that have helped me along this way; and in moments of self doubt, the comforting presence of the divine spirit has nudged me on.

and to:

- Marge for your unconditional love.

- Tom for your strength and gentle support.

- Martene for your vibe, creative input and nuttiness.

- Andrew B. for your warm hearted support.

- Dylan K. for our many lunches and your valuable feedback.

- Daniella for your enthusiasm, encouragement and research support.

- Dom for a being a loyal friend, always.

- Michele for friendship and great coaching.

- Marc S. for being a mentor and role model.

- Savannah S. for filling this journey with love and laughter.

I also acknowledge Creative Consciousness International and Steven Covey for their work and how it has contributed to this creation.

With much love, always,

Zane Green

Here's how to make sure you get the MOST value and fun from this program

✓ Put pen to paper!

Use a pen or pencil and actually write down the answers you come up with in the spaces provided – or keep a goal journal.

✓ Use your own words!

Don't get caught up in trying to make it sound 'right' or 'good', or copying what you've heard. Take time to think and express what is really true for you. What do YOU think, feel and want?

✓ Complete every step!

Complete each and every step and give yourself time to work through them completely. Have a little break between each chapter, and remember - have fun doing this!

✓ Create time and space!

Ensure you are comfortable, have enough time and have rested before engaging in these exercises. Go for making this process a comfortable and enjoyable one. Choose to see it as precious and important for you, and what matters to you!

✓ And again! REMEMBER ☺ - Put pen to paper!

Energy, clarity and connection to these exercises only occur when you write the answers down, so don't just think them out – write them out!!!

For BEST success, make a decision now:

 I will give _____ minutes per day / week to this workbook.

I will do this every day/ week at _____ time.

I have noted this in my diary.

CONTENT

Goal Setting Workbook Workout

Prelude:

Happivate Life Assessment: Getting a clear picture of where you are at now.   1-8

Main:

1. How to goal set, get your results… and have fun!   9-13

2. Defining your goal and making it measurable   14-16

3. Make your goal achievable: Part A - Getting real about what it will take   17-20

4. Make your goal achievable: Part B - Setting your milestones to achieve your goal in bite sizes   21-23

5. Getting support to achieve your goals   24-26

6. A midway progress check - Get out there and do it!   27-28

7. Overcoming obstacles, getting unstuck: PART A - Making progress on your goals   29-30

8. Overcoming obstacles, getting unstuck: PART B – Breaking down and breaking through   31-33

9. Acknowledging progress, celebrating your victories   34-36

10. Completion: Lessons learned and focus going forward   37-40

Examples and Annexures:

1. Example 1 - Goal Vision Page   41

2. Example 2 - Goal Vision Page   42

3. Annexure A - Goal Vision Page   43

4. Annexure B - Goal and Milestone Summary Sheet   44

5. Annexure C - Key Actions Page   45

Happivate Life Assessment:
Getting a clear picture of where you are at now.

Getting in touch with where you are in your life right now is the key to setting a solid foundation before embarking on setting and achieving your goals.

Whatever goals you set now will be achieved based on your current life circumstances, which need to be reflected on so that you can build on a solid base.

Take a moment now and complete this Happivate Life Assessment:

A. Your History

1. What would you say have been your 3 greatest accomplishments in your life so far?

I. _____

_____

II. _____

_____

III. _____

_____

2. What is the hardest thing in your life that you have had to overcome?

_____

_____

3. Have you worked with personal growth books, a coach or any similar one-on-one adult relationship (e.g. sports coach, piano teacher or therapist)? Please give brief details...

_____

_____

Happivate Life Assessment:
Getting a clear picture of where you are at now.

4. If you said yes to the above, what worked well for you and what did not work in the relationship(s)?

List what did NOT work well

I. _____

_____

II. _____

_____

III. _____

_____

List what DID work well

I. _____

_____

II. _____

_____

III. _____

_____

Prelude

Happivate Life Assessment:
Getting a clear picture of where you are at now.

B. About you

1. On a scale of 1 to 10, 10 being high, rate the amount of stress in your life right now.

2. What are your main causes of stress right now?

3. List three things that you are tolerating or putting up with in your life currently. (examples: broken home appliance, incomplete filing, messy room or garage, rude friends, poor lighting, tight shoes, dented car, job dissatisfaction, dead plants, broken equipment, old appliances, pain in your body etc.)

I.

II.

III.

Happivate Life Assessment:
Getting a clear picture of where you are at now.

List 3 adjectives that describe you at your <u>best</u>

I. _____

_____

II. _____

_____

III. _____

_____

List 3 adjectives that describe you at your <u>worst</u>

I. _____

_____

II. _____

_____

III. _____

_____

What motivates you?

_____

_____

Happivate Life Assessment:
Getting a clear picture of where you are at now.

C. Your goals and coaching

Note: Rate how well this area of your life is out of 10, 10 being "excellent".

1. RATE the key areas of your life, in terms of how well these areas are going currently. *(Rate between 1 and 10)*	Score *(Where 10 is "excellent")*	Tick the top 3 areas you most wish to improve.
Health & Wellness		
Personal Relationship		
Wealth & Finances		
Self Character & Personal Growth		
Family and Home		
Business & Career		
Friends & Leisure Time		
Spiritual & Community		
Administration (Banking, Filing, Tax, Legal, etc)		
Other (One other key area that is important to me in my life)		

Considering the ratings, your current situation and what you most want, now answer the following questions:

2. What are the 3 biggest changes you want to make in your life in the next 3 months?

I. _____

_____

II. _____

_____

III. _____

_____

 **Prelude**

Happivate Life Assessment:
Getting a clear picture of where you are at now.

3. What are the 3 biggest changes you want to make in your life in the next 3 years?

I. _____

_____

II. _____

_____

III. _____

_____

4. What do you most want to achieve and do you feel ready for it – what goal do you most wish to achieve in the next 3 to 6 months?

_____

_____

5. List at least one person who is best suited to be your "goal buddy"! (NOTE: A "Goal Buddy" is a friend or colleague you choose and share your goal with, and then request their support to achieve your goal.)

_____

_____

6. What would you like your "goal buddy" and/ or coach to do if you fall behind on your goals?

_____

_____

Prelude

Happivate Life Assessment:
Getting a clear picture of where you are at now.

7. If you reach the age of 105 and continue to live your life and spend your time and money the way you do right now, what regrets do you think you will have? (Do not include things from the past-only things you will regret if you continue on your exact present path.)

D. Coach Readiness

1. TICK the key statements, in terms of how much you agree with them.

	Disagree	Somewhat Agree	Agree	Strongly Agree
I am committed to and need and want to improve my life.	☐	☐	☐	☐
I am not looking for a "quick fix"; I understand coaching is an ongoing process for creating changes in my life.	☐	☐	☐	☐
I am open to honest feedback and candid assessments.	☐	☐	☐	☐
I am the only one who can make my life better; I acknowledge my life will remain the same unless I make my goals a priority.	☐	☐	☐	☐
I accept responsibility for my choices and actions and do not expect anyone to "fix" me.	☐	☐	☐	☐
I view workbook and/ or personal coaching as a worthwhile investment in "me", which will support me to achieve my goals.	☐	☐	☐	☐
I am ready to prioritise time and money and make this investment in what matters most to me!	☐	☐	☐	☐

2. How will you know when you are receiving value (i.e. your money's worth) from the coaching process?

Prelude

Happivate Life Assessment:
Getting a clear picture of where you are at now.

3. YES! I will share my Happivate Goal Assessment information with my "Goal Buddy" by _____ (Date); and I commit to completing this goal by: _____(Date).

What is the most valuable thing you got from completing this exercise?

_____

_____

01

How to goal set, get your
results...
and have fun!

Nothing happens unless first we dream.

- Carl Sandburg

Deciding on a goal - Daring to speak what you really want!

'I already know what my goal is!'
Skip "Exercise 1A" and go to "Exercise 1B" below it.

'I am still choosing my goal' or 'I need help formulating my goal'. (Stay tuned.)
Complete "Exercise1A" and then go on to "Exercise 1B".

Exercise 1A

Most of us have dreams and goals that we think about, fantasize about, even talk about, yet never actually write down or consider making happen. The difference between a dream and a goal is that a goal is something we are doing something about, something we are pursuing. A dream on the other hand is something we wish we could have or achieve, but never risk to actually act upon.

So, take a minute now and list 5 goals, or dreams that you have only been thinking about, or even made some progress on. The key here is that they are goals that you really (read: really really really) wish for and are excited about, ones that you may have been thinking about for years...

List 5 of your biggest and most exciting "possible" goals here:

1) _____

_____

2) _____

_____

3) _____

_____

4) _____

5) _____

_____

Now,

1. *Pick the one of the five that is most exciting and most achievable, one that you wish to focus on and circle it.*
2. *What goal (or milestone that supports a larger goal) do you choose to commit to completing in the next 3 months?*

> TIP: If your goal is so big it may take years to complete, then consider a goal that is a step towards achieving this BIG goal...

Write YOUR GOAL **down here:**

_____

_____

> And remember to add the date by when you commit to completing it!

NOTE: *If you are still a little stuck on clarifying your goal, see "Annexure A" at the back of the book for a full goal questionnaire.*

Exercise 1B

Ok, so you know what your goal is. Congratulations. Making sure you set out in the right direction is as important as your speed. This exercise will help you build energy, motivation and power to achieve your goal.

(Honesty moment! Do you really want this goal or is it something you feel obligated to do? If you are not sure, complete/ repeat "Exercise1A".)

Write down 5 reasons why you want this goal:

1) _____

_____

2) _____

_____

3) _____

_____

4) _____

_____

5) _____

_____

The more reasons why you want your goal, the greater motivation and will power you will have. Stretch yourself a little ☺ - if you have more reasons - keep writing! Make sure you have all your reasons down:

1) _____

_____

2) _____

_____

3) _____

_____

4) _____

_____

5) _____

_____

6) _____

_____

7) _____

_____

8) _____

_____

9) _____

_____

and even 10) _____

_____

Step 01 is now complete
Well Done

02

Defining your goal and making it measurable.

Don't bunt. Aim out of the ball park. Aim for the company of immortals.

- David Ogilvy

Exercise 2A

So now we will ensure your goal is clear, defined and measurable.

Take a moment and visualise yourself having achieved your goal…
- ✓ What do you see?
- ✓ What do you feel?
- ✓ Is anyone with you, and if so who?

What will the indictors be that you have achieved your goal?
How will you know it is complete?

Examples of goals and tangible indicators...

Example One:

1. My goal is to get a new job that fulfils me and meets my financial needs.
2. My indicators that I have achieved this are:
> *a. I completed course certificate saying I passed the course in line with my new job.*
> *b. I will be feeling more competent and skilled in what I studied,*
> *c. I will have a job offer based on the skills I got from the course, which meets my financial needs.*

Example Two:

1. My goal is to lose weight and get into shape.
2. My indicators that I have achieved this are:
> *a. I wear clothes 3 sizes less and I have lost 20 pounds.*
> *b. I feel comfortable and good about myself when I go out.*
> *c. I can comfortably walk 3 miles a few times per week.*

PUT PEN TO PAPER>>>

Write down 3 tangible indicators that will tell you that you have achieved your goal.

1) _____

_____

2) _____

_____

3) _____

_____

Now write an approximate date and time by when you wish to complete your goal:

_____

_____

Exercise 2B

To further empower, motivate and support you, set aside time to gather some pictures that represent you achieving your goal.

✓ Get hold of some old magazines or visit http://images.google.com, and collect 3-4 pictures that represent you achieving your goal. You will need these pictures to complete your "Goal Vision Page Template" which is annexure A at the back of the workbook.

✓ Don't wait, do this NOW if you are able.

(If you don't have time to do this now, make a date with yourself sometime this week for half an hour to do it.)

Step 02 is complete
You are already moving closer to achieving your goal.

03

Make your goal achievable:
Part A - Getting real about what it will take

It isn't where you come from,
it's where you're going that counts.

- Ella Fitzgerald

When clarifying and committing to a goal we need to get "real" about our goal(s). How much of a stretch is this goal, is making time for it, or completing it going take something extra, what obstacles will I encounter, who will I need agreement or support from? Take a moment now and complete the exercises below to support you in getting realistic about your goal.

REMEMBER:
Your goal should be an exciting challenge, not a walk in the park or an impossible hurdle. If your goal is too easy or too challenging, how could you adjust it to make it more realistic? As much as going for big goals is thrilling, it is also important to establish a foundation of strength within yourself. It is better to achieve some steps, than plan big ones and achieve nothing!

Exercise 3A

How much time (in hours) will you need to invest in your goal?

_____

_____

How much money will you need to invest in your goal?

_____

_____

List the top 3 people who could best support you to achieve your goal:

1) _____

_____

2) _____

_____

3) _____

_____

Also, what parts of your life are you willing to give less time, money and energy to in order to prioritise this goal, let's look at this next exercise...

List the top 3 obstacles you will need to overcome to achieve your goal?

1) _____

_____

2) _____

_____

3) _____

_____

Exercise 3B

The thing you could do (or stop doing), that you are willing to do (or stop doing), that will free up the TIME you need to achieve your goal is:

_____

_____

The thing you could do (or stop doing), that you are willing to do (or stop doing), that will free up the MONEY you need to achieve your goal is:

_____

_____

The thing you could do (or stop doing), that you are willing to do (or stop doing), that will free up the ENERGY you need to achieve your goal is:

_____

_____

Is this a goal you are willing to commit yourself to?

YES	NO

STEP 03 Part A is now complete.

Good work !

04

Making your goal achievable:
<u>Part B</u> - Setting milestones
to achieve your
goal in bite sizes!

It is better to fall short of a high mark than to reach a low one.

- H. C. Payne

Making your goal achievable:
<u>Part B</u> – Setting milestones to achieve your goal in bite sizes!

NOTE!!!   *Milestones are mini-goals that you need to achieve along the way to achieving your overall goal.*

You may want to achieve this goal as quickly as possible. The reality is that time, energy, money, busy lives AND most importantly, motivation are all important factors. If you are going for a big goal, break it down into manageable pieces… It will seem much less overwhelming and each milestone achieved will actually increase your energy and motivation for tackling the next milestone.

Exercise 4A

Take a moment now and think about what you will need to do in order to complete your goal, what are the steps along the way? List whatever comes to mind and write it down here:

1) _____

_____

2) _____

_____

3) _____

_____

4) _____

_____

5) _____

_____

6) _____

_____

04

Making your goal achievable:
Part B – Setting milestones to achieve your goal in bite sizes!

7) _____

_____

8) _____

_____

9) _____

_____

10) _____

_____

Exercise 4B

Considering the list of steps in Exercise 4A, now try and group them into 6 key milestones or mini-goals.

Be sure to check that you have given yourself a clear achievement date and time for each milestone – YES be specific to the minute for every one of them.

Assigning dates to each milestone will support you to track your progress and stay on track!

> NOTE: This is a KEY step!!!– The power of this exercise is actually writing down up to 6 milestones with their due dates.

>>>PLEASE turn to the back of the book "Annexure B" to fill in your 6 milestones with dates

STEP 04 is now complete.
WELL DONE!

05

Getting support to achieve your goals

Arriving at one goal is the starting point to another.

- John Dewey

05 Getting support to achieve your goals

Sharing your goal is key to supporting your success. The key benefits of sharing your goal with those close to you are:

✓ There is a natural pressure to complete your goal after you have told someone.
✓ Telling people about your goals affirms to yourself that you are serious about this goal.
✓ People often offer resources or support if they know what your goal is.
✓ Those close to you may experience changes from you that will leave them uncertain or resist supporting you if you haven't shared your new goal and the reasons why it is important to you, with them.

NOTE: Just share and request support from a few key people, talking too much about your goal may also waste the time and energy you could put into completing your goal.

EXTRA SPECIALNOTE: When sharing your goal, be sure to share the most important reasons WHY you want this goal – that way people understand and can support you more powerfully... And remember to request the kind of support you need.

Exercise 5

1. Name of the person who can best support you:

2. The kind of support you request from them and how often or when:

3. The date by when you will speak with them:

05 Getting support to achieve your goals

1. Name of one other person who can best support you:

_____

2. The kind of support you request from them and how often or when:

_____

_____

3. The date by when you will speak with them:

_____

STEP 05 is now complete.

06

A midway progress check -
Get out there and do it!

If you don't know where you are going,
you can never get lost.

- Herb Cohen

A midway progress check –
Get out there and do it!

Celebrate! Each milestone took energy and commitment to get to, ensure you give yourself a pause and acknowledge what you have accomplished so far, and what you have not.

Exercise 6

Run through this checklist now and see how far you have come:

☐ *My goal is clear and measurable; I know what the indicators are that I have achieved it.*

☐ *I am clear about why I want this goal, what it will give me and what about it inspires and motivates me!*

☐ *I have set a date by when I will achieve my goal and broken the goal into smaller milestones and set dates for each milestone.*

☐ *This goal and timeframe is realistic and I am committed to achieving it.*

☐ *I have written my goal down and stuck it up somewhere visible.*

☐ *I commit to celebrating my progress at each milestone and having fun.*

☐ *I have shared my goal with a friend/ colleague and requested their support!*

Now list anything from above that is incomplete and still needs to be done:

_____

_____

_____

KEY ACTION: Complete anything from the previous chapters that still needs to be completed – NOW ☺

Step 06 is complete.

Setting goals and milestones and then achieving them is a skill, so no matter what you do, just by completing these exercises and setting and achieving a small goal is already developing your ability to set and achieve goals. Practice makes perfect!

07

Overcoming obstacles,
getting unstuck:

PART A - making progress on
your goals

The greatest danger for most of us is not
that our aim is too high and we miss it,
but that it is too low and we reach it.

Michelangelo-

07 Overcoming obstacles, getting unstuck:
PART A - making progress on your goals.

At some point we inevitably get stuck, either we fail to even start our goal, or we hit some unanticipated situation that drains or stops us and we feel like or do give up. The key to getting unstuck is making a decision or taking action, even if we don't feel like it.

In this section we deal with overcoming internal obstacles. Here's a list of common reasons we don't set goals or give up somewhere along the way...

1. We tell ourselves "White Lies"

- We tell ourselves we don't have the time (I'm too busy) or money to do this, if you are reading this then you have some access to time and/or money.
- It is not a matter of having time or money, it is a matter of whether you are willing to spend the money and time you currently allocate to other things to your goals?
- Take a moment now and ask yourself - Where am I currently spending time/ money/ energy, that I could spend on my important goals?

Commit to a small amount of time and/or money you can allocate each day or week to this goal.

2. Tomorrow never comes: We put our goals into a vague future.

- Many of us tell ourselves we will action our goal sometime in the future and never actually start.
- Unless you have set a specific date for when you will start this goal it will sit in your head (and heart) as vague and nagging on your energy.
- Make a decision now about your goal, either let it go forever, commit to it now, or commit to a date when you will start.

Setting a goal and taking one tiny step is an achievement in itself worth celebrating.

3. We forget to have fun

- We do not take time to acknowledge what we have done or celebrate our progress.

08

Overcoming obstacles, getting unstuck:
PART B - breaking down and breaking through.

The world makes way for the man who knows where he is going.

- *Ralph Waldo Emerson*

08 Overcoming obstacles, getting unstuck:
PART B – breaking down and breaking through.

In the previous section we looked at the common reasons why we get stuck and how to get out. That said, there are times where we simply feel like giving up and there is nothing more to give.

A "break down" is that point where we simply run out of energy, motivation or the will to complete our goal. We have done all the normal things and we simply feel beaten, tired or like completely giving up.

The good news is that this is "normal" and we all have these moments which may last for a minute or a month; we don't often hear people speak of them, but we all do have them.

The bad news is that this is a very real and challenging obstacle and we call it a "break down". This is the most common cause for abandoning our dreams, goals and aspirations, so if your goal really matters to you – pay attention.

Most of us don't like to admit to ourselves or our friends/ supporters that we feel this way, it feels like failure and like quitting – so we avoid feeling it.

So, make a note of this section and go through the exercise below if and when you reach this point, experiencing a "break down".

So how do we get past a "break down"?

Only engage in this exercise when you feel like you are in a "break down"

1. Admit to yourself that you are in a goal "break down"; that this will happen sometimes and it is ok.
2. Express your feelings/ thoughts.
3. Share these feelings/ thoughts with a friend who is a good listener (preferably someone who will just listen and "hear" you without trying to solve your problems for you).
4. Re-read what your goal is and why you want it.
5. Make a decision: What decision or action could you take now to take you one small step forward?

Exercise 8

Remember, the power of this exercise is in doing it, not just reading it or thinking about doing it in your head!

1. Yes, I am in a break down ☐ (tick here)
2. Right now, I am thinking/ feeling this about my goal or this part of it:

_____

_____

_____

(and take a few deep breaths in and out...)

3. I will call _____ (friend/ colleague) and share this with them by _____ (date and time).

4. I have re-read my goal and why I want it. ☐ (tick here)

5. What decision or action could you take now to take you one small step forward?

Action/ Decision is:

_____

_____

By date and time:

_____

Step 08 is complete
WELL DONE!

09

Acknowledging progress, celebrating your victories.

What we think, determines what happens to us,
so if we want to change our lives,
we need to stretch our minds.

- *Wayne Dyer*

If you have gotten this far in the Workbook Workout then WELL DONE!

It is so easy to focus on what still needs to be done, or how you could have gotten here faster or in some better way. STOP.

You are here and it took something for you to get here! You have overcome obstacles, engaged in your goals and got this far. Each milestone, so far, took energy and commitment to get you here, ensure you give yourself a break and acknowledge what you have accomplished so far.

Exercise 9

List the top 5 tasks, milestones or obstacles you have completed so far:

1) _____

_____

2) _____

_____

3) _____

_____

4) _____

_____

5) _____

_____

What has been the greatest challenge you have had to overcome to get this far:

_____

_____

I am most grateful to myself in having gotten this far, for:

_____

_____

I will call _____ (friend/colleague) and share this with them by _____ (date and time).

What decision or action could you take now to celebrate how far you have come?

Action/ Decision is:

_____

_____

By date and time:

_____

Step 09 is complete.

10

Completion:
Lessons learned and focus going forward.

Life takes on meaning when you become motivated, set goals and charge after them in an unstoppable manner.

- Les Brown

Dear Goal Setter and friend,

Well done to making it to the final stage. A quick recap of what we covered:

- How to goal set – setting goals the easy way.

- Making your goal measurable.

- Making your goal achievable: Part A - Getting real about what it will take.

- Making your goal achievable: Part B - Setting milestones.

- Getting support from friends or colleagues.

- Getting out there – A midway progress check.

- Overcoming obstacles, getting unstuck: PART A - making progress on your goals.

- Overcoming obstacles, getting unstuck: PART B – breaking down and breaking through.

- Celebrating and acknowledging what you have achieved.

As I sat and prepared this Workbook Workout I was struck by my many challenges in managing and focusing my own energy, and sometimes failing and feeling depleted too. It is with many years of my own trials, as well as those I have supported along the way, and countless hours of research that I have compiled these key essential lessons, and have learned to channel my energy into the things that energize me!

I thank you and am grateful for your participation in this program. Please do provide us with feedback at www.happivate.com/workbookfeedback.php

Please now complete the final step 10.

And again I must stress, there is power in actually writing out and doing these exercises, this is where the real value lies!

Completion:
Lessons learned and focus going forward.

Take a few moments now and complete this final exercise to enhance and cement the value you have gained:

Exercise 10

The 3 most important lessons I have learned about goal setting and achieving during this Workbook Workout are:

1) _____

_____

2) _____

_____

3) _____

_____

The one thing I commit to continue doing daily or weekly is:

_____

_____

_____

The most valuable thing I gained from engaging with this Workbook Workout is:

_____

_____

_____

Time to Share!

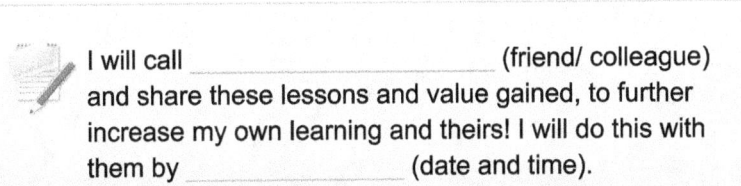

I will call _____ (friend/ colleague) and share these lessons and value gained, to further increase my own learning and theirs! I will do this with them by _____ (date and time).

Step 10 is complete.

The Happivate Team wishes you continued success and happiness!

EXAMPLE 1 - My Goal Vision Page

My goal is (Defined with a due date)

TO FEEL GOOD ABOUT MYSELF AND MY PHYSICAL BODY

Why am I doing this? (Most important and exciting reasons)

1) SO I CAN FEEL POSITIVE ABOUT HOW I LOOK AND HOW MY BODY FEELS

2) TO FEEL FREE AND GOOD ABOUT BEING SEEN IN A PICTURE AT THE BEACH AND LOOK GOOD WHEN I GO OUT

3) BECAUSE I AM TIRED OF THINGS AS THEY ARE AND KNOW THAT IF I DON'T DO SOMETHING ABOUT IT I WILL JUST CARRY ON FEELING GUILTY AND UNHAPPY WITH MY WEIGHT AND FITNESS

4) SO I CAN FEEL ENERGIZED HEALTHY AND SEXY 😊

5)

I will know I have achieved this goal when (Tangible indicators)

1) I CAN FIT INTO A SIZE 32 PANTS COMFORTABLY

2) I AM DOING EXERCISE 3 TIMES PER WEEK AND FEEL MORE ENERGIZED

3) WHEN I AM OUT IN PUBLIC I FEEL GOOD ABOUT HOW I LOOK AND FEEL IN MY BODY

Encouraging pictures that represent me completing this goal

EXAMPLE 2 - My Goal Vision Page

My goal is (Defined with a due date)

TO MOVE TO A JOB THAT FULFILS ME AND PAYS ME WHAT I AM WORTH BY 01 SEPTEMBER THIS YEAR

Why am I doing this? (Most important and exciting reasons)

1) SO I CAN FEEL POSITIVE ABOUT WHAT I DO

2) TO SPEND MORE WORK TIME DOING THINGS THAT I LOVE DOING AND AM GOOD AT

3) BECAUSE I AM TIRED OF THINGS AS THEY ARE AND KNOW THAT IF I DON'T DO SOMETHING ABOUT IT I WILL JUST CARRY ON IN THIS JOB WHICH IS SUCKING THE LIFE OUT OF ME!

4) SO I CAN FEEL MY LIFE IS ON TRACK AND I AM FULFILLED!

5)

I will know I have achieved this goal when (Tangible indicators)

1) I HAVE STUDIED AND COMPLETED MY COACHING DIPLOMA

2) I AM EARNING AT LEAST $5 000 PER MONTH

3) MY CLIENTS ARE FEEDING BACK THAT THEY ARE VERY SATISFIED WITH THE VALUE THEY GET!

Encouraging pictures that represent me completing this goal

 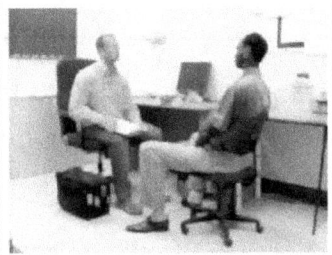

ANNEXURE A - My Goal Vision Page

TIP: Copy this page and put it somewhere where you will see it every day!

My goal is (Defined with a due date)

Why am I doing this? (Most important and exciting reasons)

1)

2)

3)

4)

5)

I will know I have achieved this goal when (Tangible indicators)

1)

2)

3)

Encouraging pictures that represent me completing this goal

Annexure B - Goal and Milestone Summary Sheet

My Goal is:

Milestone 01

Due Date:

Milestone 02

Due Date:

Milestone 03

Due Date:

Milestone 04

Due Date:

Milestone 05

Due Date:

Final Goal!!

Milestone 06

Due Date:

ANNEXURE C - Key Actions Page

TIP: As you go through the workbook capture any ideas/ tasks and things to do here!

Task	Due Date